TABLE OF CONTENTS

Page

ACRONYMS.. iii

ILLUSTRATIONS v

TABLES vii

CHAPTER 1 INTRODUCTION 1

A. POLITICAL VIOLENCE DEFINED 3
B. CHAPTER-BY-CHAPTER SUMMARY...9
Chapter 1: Introduction 9
Chapter 2: Literature Review...9
Chapter 3: Research Methodology..10
Chapter 4: Analysis..10
Chapter 5: Child Soldiers...11
Chapter 6: Conclusion..11

CHAPTER 2 LITERATURE REVIEW 13

Introduction...13
A. CENTRAL RESEARCH 13
I. Terrorism or Insurgency? 13
Merari's "Terrorism as a Strategy of Insurgency"..13
The Collier-Hoeffler Model...15
"On the Incidence of Civil War in Africa" by Paul Collier and Anke Hoeffler............18
Sambanis' "Using Case Studies to Expand the Theory of Civil War" 19
II. Violence Against Noncombatants 21
Child Soldiers..21
B. STRENGTHS AND WEAKNESSES OF THE LITERATURE 22

CHAPTER 3 RESEARCH METHODOLOGY 28

Introduction...28
Goals and Explanation of Criteria..29
Independent Variables 31
    Economic variables: GDP, Growth, Education 32
    Population 33
    Diasporas...34
    Ethnicity and Social Fragmentation, and Polarization............................34
    Political Institutions 35
Conclusion 35

i

CHAPTER 4 WEST AFRICAN POLITICAL VIOLENCE ANALYSIS 37

Introduction...37
A. CASE STUDIES OF LIBERIA, CÔTE D'IVOIRE AND SIERRA LEONE..........37
Liberia...37
    (Data for Liberia based on my own ascertainments, not from Sambanis)**Error! Bookmark not define**
Côte d'Ivoire 39
Sierra Leone 43
B. SIGNIFICANCE 47

CHAPTER 5 CHILD SOLDIERS 49

Introduction...49
Why Children Fight 51
Children Committing Political Violence 54

CHAPTER 6 CONCLUSION...57

A. CURRENT US STRATEGY IN WEST AFRICA 57
National Security Strategy for Africa 58
B. THE UNITED STATES' COMMITMENT TO CURB POLITICAL VIOLENCE
IN WEST AFRICA 60
C. CONCLUSION 62

GLOSSARY 64

REFERENCE LIST 65

ACRONYMS

AIDS	Acquired Immune Deficiency Syndrome
aka	Also known as
AU	African Union
BCEAO	Central Bank of West African States
CFA	Centrale Franc d'Afrique (common currency of ECOWAS)
CIA	Central Intelligence Agency
CH	Collier-Hoeffler Model developed for the World Bank in 2000
DRC	Democratic Republic of the Congo
ECOWAS	Economic Community Of West African States
ECOMIL	Economic Community Of West African States Military
ECOMOG	Economic Community of West African States Military Observer Group
FBI	Federal Bureau of Investigation
GDP	Gross Domestic Product
IMET	International Military Educational Training
FTO	Foreign Terrorist Organization
JCET	Joint Combined Exchange Training
JCS	Joint Chiefs of Staff
LCS	Liberia, Cotê d'Ivoire and Sierra Leone
LURD	Liberians United for Reconciliation and Democracy
NATO	North Atlantic Treaty Organization
NPFL	National Patriotic Front of Liberia
NSS	National Security Strategy
OAU	Organization of African Unity

OEF	Operation Enduring Freedom (Afghanistan)
OIF	Operation Iraqi Freedom
UBL	Usama Bin Laden
USEUCOM	United States European Command
US	United States
USA	United States Army
USAF	Unites States Air Force
USMC	United States Marine Corps
UN	United Nations
UNAMSIL	United Nations Mission in Sierra Leone
UNMIL	United Nation Mission in Liberia
UNCTAD	United Nations Conference on Trade and Development
SADC	South African Development Community
SSA	Sub-Saharan Africa
WA	West Africa

ILLUSTRATIONS

Page

Figure 1. .... Map of West Africa...1

.

TABLES

Page

Table 1.   A Basic Classification of Political Violence (Merari)...........................16
Table 2.   CH Model Applied to Liberia..37
Table 3.   CH Model Applied to Côte d'Ivoire 39
Table 4.   CH Model Applied to Sierra Leone...42

CHAPTER 1

INTRODUCTION

The threat of terror to U.S interests in Africa is concrete, rising, and discernible. The probability of another attack on Americans on African soil is high. The United States has begun to recognize this reality and to give counterterrorism higher priority in U.S. foreign policy approaches to the continent. To be effective, policymakers will have to contend seriously with the very factors that attract terrorists: weak state partners, deep economic marginality and alienation, ethnic and religious fissures on a continent that is home to 300 million Muslims, and fragile governance with often weak protections of democratic and human rights. For this reason, security programs cannot drive the U.S. response alone; it also requires sustained attention to economic development, human rights, and democratization.

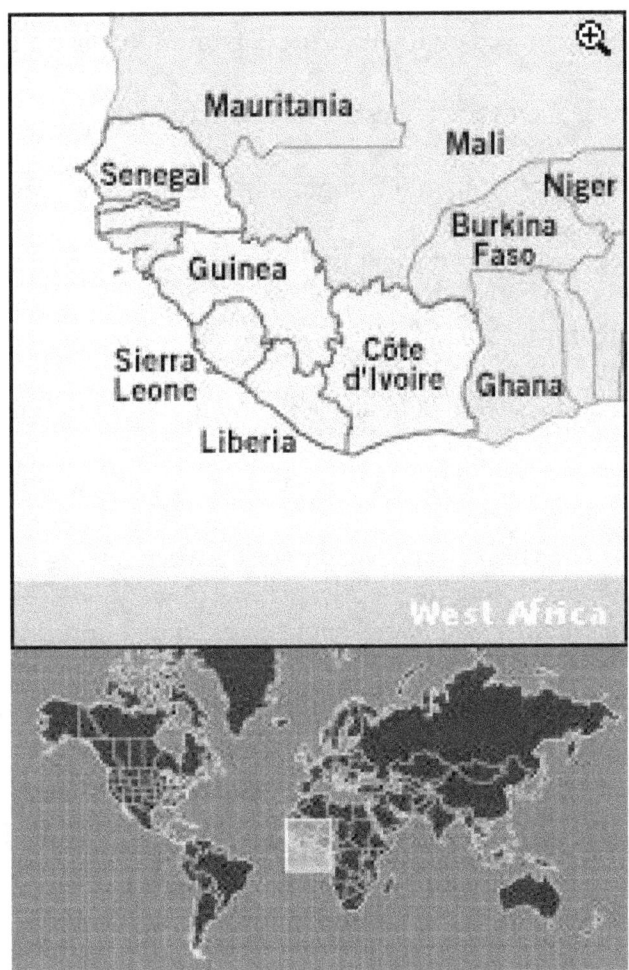

Figure 1. Map of West Africa

General James Jones of U.S. European Command and NATO said, "I think Africa is a continent that is going to be of very, very significant interest in the 21st century."

In West Africa regional conflicts have waged for decades, driven by greed and political disintegration. The late 1990s saw the culmination of the diamond and corruption fuelled rebellion in Sierra Leone that had been going on for a decade. At the start of 2000 a recently signed peace agreement in Sierra Leone was on the brink of failure. Liberia, nominally at peace after its own war in the first half of the decade but little more than a façade of a state benefiting no one but its gangster-like regime, was still fomenting conflict in all of its neighbors (Sierra Leone, Guinea and Côte D'Ivoire) and was itself edging towards a renewed civil war. Côte d'Ivoire too, once a beacon of prosperity and stability, was increasingly beset by its own internal political troubles that were to develop into armed conflict in 2002. Nigeria, the regional hegemon, was ruled for most of the 1990s by a repressive and corrupt military regime that thrived in part on fomenting ethnic and religious tensions.

Many African economies were quite damaged by the Western imposed economic policies of the 1970-1980s (Osei, 2002). Many governments are now at the mercy of anyone with a few bucks. They have to make a choice between buying medicine for school children and paying interests on loans that were extended to corrupt regimes during the Cold War by western banks. Countries like Liberia, Côte d'Ivoire, and Sierra Leone had to scramble for decades to pay for loans extended to Samuel Doe, Houphouet-Boigny, Momo (respective former leaders of the mentioned countries) and others whose most important credentials were to be "anti-communists." Now, these impoverished countries are breeding grounds for terrorism and political violence. Liberia is home to every gangster dealing with drugs (for the thousands of addicted fighters), money to buy blood diamonds and arms for the multitude of renegade armed groups the regime works with all across the continent.

Africa's wars in the 1990s were all very different in their specifics. But they shared a number of important characteristics. First, one of the main underlying causes of these wars was the weakness, the corruption, the high level of militarization, and in some cases the complete collapse, of the states involved. Secondly, they all involved multiple belligerents fighting for a multiplicity of often shifting economic and political motivations. Thirdly, they all had serious regional dimensions and regional implications. And fourthly they were all remarkable for the brutality of the tactics (ranging from mass murder and ethnic cleansing, to amputation, starvation, forced labor, rape and cannibalism) used by belligerents to secure their strategic objectives.

A. POLITICAL VIOLENCE DEFINED

The factors of violence in West Africa, on the surface, seem sparse at best. The tumultuous issues of famine, poverty, natural resource ownership and race relations might distract an observer of this part of the world, let alone this western-most part of this vast continent. However, as one begins to delve into what political violence actually means, how it is propagated and its effects in West Africa, one may begin to see that this form of violence indeed exists. At the outset, these questions must be posed: What is the likelihood that political violence or the threat of this violence exists against civilians/noncombatants? Why is there violence against noncombatants in this region? In this thesis I will look at three countries in which I believe political violence, and perhaps terrorism, are prevalent. Liberia, Côte d'Ivoire and Sierra Leone (LCS) all have wrestled with political violence especially over the last decade. Political and social violence ravage communities destroy lives and property and grossly violate the sanctity of life. However, political violence is the violence that is ignited and enabled for political motives. The prize for this brutal contestation is the control of state power. As long as power is in question and is there for the taking, political violence will rage on. Because political violence threatens the state, international diplomacy has some remedy for it. Organizing elections, for example, to transform the violence into a more noble and acceptable competition and the imposition of sanctions on noncompliant groups have been used to end political violence.

In Sierra Leone's political struggle there was less and less manipulation of social difference, that is, the political forces at work, violent and non-violent, seemed to not affect Sierra Leonean social thought in a way that saw the rebels as necessarily an affliction. The conflict did not polarize the society nor did it thrust itself into the minds of different political and social groups. The political slogan was still clear—that the rebels are fighting to stamp out governmental corruption and to establish good political ascendancy and that neighboring Liberia's Charles Taylor was to blame. The violators of human rights are not associated with any one tribe. It must be noted that political hierarchy is most often perpetuated along tribal lines and preference is most often given to those that come from that tribe. They are essentially members of groups that are held responsible for their crimes. The groups themselves are political and military entities whose members are drawn from every tribe. Political violence is driven by interest while social violence is driven by need. It is this interweaving of one's interest and one's need that begins to shed light upon why violence occurs. In social violence people are fighting

4

to exist. Social violence first assaults the mind and plants the sense of insecurity. We all desire security for our person and our property. Thereafter, it forces its victim to begin to wonder about the dignity of life; thus leading to dehumanization of ones nature and others. Your memory, a composite of your individual and collective identity is wounded and at times collapses during these periods of violence. In other words, social violence strips people of their humanity and replaces it with inhumanity. As long as that society loses its sense of humanity, violence becomes commonplace.

The distinction between the two does not suggest that they always exist in separate time and space. In fact they almost always inspire each other. Long political struggle that exploits social difference soon transforms into social violence; while more social violence are often the exploitative and manipulative gimmicks of politicians.

Politically motivated violence is commonly referred to by the terms terrorism, rebellion, war, conquest, revolution, oppression, tyranny, and many others. In general, it can be defined as committing violent actions against others with the intended purpose of effecting a change in their actions.

It has been said that "violence is the last option of a desperate man." Politically motivated violence has been used throughout history to greater and lesser effect by virtually every people in existence today. The root causes of this form of violence may be traced to several fundamental factors economic stratification, moral dissociation, and/or psychological dysfunction. The validity of the reasons for the violence are often highly dependent on who is doing the judging. It is important to note that the validity, or rightness/wrongness of the violence cannot reliably be judged by affected parties. This is due not to an inherent flaw in judgement but to the competing concern for the self preservation of the ego. Political violence may then have linkages to terrorism or they might be synonymous. This thesis discusses the factors of political violence in West Africa but it is also important to address that terrorism is often embedded within political violence.

On the surface, the popular definition of 'terrorism' represents a shift from previous means of defining an enemy, that is, from territorial or cultural disputes over ideology or religion, to the open acts of violence against the public. Many people dispute this definition however as ideological and simplistic, arguing instead that 'terrorism' is simply another in a long lists of enemy terms — that underneath any current conflict lies the same materialistic and ethnocentric reasons of which most past wars were based. The use of the terms *terrorism* and *terrorist* are politically weighted, and are often used for a polarizing effect, where 'terrorism' becomes simply a relativist term for the violence committed by an enemy, from the point of view of the attacked. Because of the political nature of some struggles, 'terrorism' can become identified as simply any violence committed against established institutions.

Annette Hübschle expounds that, "defining terrorism has been a particularly difficult task on the African continent. In fact, most legal drafters stay clear of defining it but rather describe an 'act of terror' or 'terrorist activity'. The 35th Ordinary Session of the Heads of State and Government adopted the Organization of African Unity Convention on the Prevention and Combating of Terrorism (the Algiers Convention) in July 1999. With the exception of Zambia and Zimbabwe, all other SADC countries have signed and/or ratified and/or deposited the Algiers Convention."

The rebels in Cote d'Ivoire are terrorists that aggressively use political violence. They are holding millions of people hostage to fulfill their political ambitions. When Charles Taylor was the President in Liberia, he was heading nothing but a terrorist organization because by force of arms, intimidation and torture, it took the whole country hostage using political violence. Blaise (president of Burkina Faso—a neighboring state), a close friend of the now-exiled Taylor, is helping the expansion of state terrorism and violence in West Africa by engaging in similar practices (Dukule).

The violence committed by state combatants is also considered more acceptable than that of the 'terrorist,' who by definition refuses to follow the established laws of war, and therefore cannot share in the acceptance given to political violence. Thus the term is impossible to apply by its rational definition — states who engage in warfare often do so outside of the laws of war and often carry out violence against civilian populations, yet rarely receive the label of "terrorist." This is the essence of political violence in West Africa. The common public distinction between state political violence and terrorism is based on a perception that terrorism targets noncombatants as a consistent policy, and therefore more irrational than state violence, which is assumed to be more considerate of human life, or at least does not consistently pursue unarmed civilian targets with the same zeal.

History does not always bear this out, however, and language reflects this: few would question that deliberate attacks on civilian refugee columns and camps is an attempt to induce terror in the enemy population and is therefore a terrorist act. As such the most accurate definition of "terrorism" must be based in its abstract nature as a term for characterizing the violence of an enemy as conforming to an immoral code of conduct.

How serious is the US about fighting political violence and terrorism will be demonstrated when, along with targeting Iraq, it also looks at the small-town bandits and dictators in "insignificants countries" that have ceased to have any "strategic interest" but can still cause serious harm to the national interest of the US and World Peace. Support for the US-led coalition against terrorism continues to grow throughout Africa. Many African leaders recognize that their countries have become a breeding ground for international terrorists. Similarly, many African leaders have come to recognize that by definition, they are supporting and running their own brand of terrorism and because of this they are now aware that the US might do something about it.

Senegal has been another leader in the African response to terrorism. Senegal's central bank and regional banks based in Dakar have modified regulations to block terrorist funding. Senegal has also created a regional counterterrorism intelligence center with assistance from the U.S. Senegal's President, Abdoulaye Wade is working with other African leaders to adopt the African Pact Against Terrorism. The pact would expand the African anti-terrorism agreement adopted in 1999 in response to the U.S. embassy bombings. More African countries must follow the lead of Senegal if they are to curb political violence and terrorism in their country.

International unity against terrorism is essential. In the words of President Bush, "The civilized world is rallying to America's side. They understand that if this terror goes unpunished, their own cities, their own citizens may be next." Former Assistant Secretary of State Susan Rice said,"I am sure you have heard, as I have, many times since

September 11, the familiar refrain, that it is quite a shame that Africa will now get fewer resources and zero attention in the context of the new focus on terrorism. And while I think we all would acknowledge the conventional wisdom underlying that sentiment, I can think of no outcome that would be more shortsighted and, indeed, more dangerous if we are not just to fight, but [also] ultimately to win the global war on terror. That is because, in my judgment, Africa is unfortunately the world's soft underbelly for global terrorism. Al-Qaeda and other terrorist cells are active throughout East, Southern, and West Africa, not to mention North Africa. These organizations hide throughout Africa. They plan, finance, train for, and execute terrorist operations in many parts of Africa, not just from Sudan and Somalia."

B. CHAPTER-BY-CHAPTER SUMMARY

Chapter 1: Introduction

An initial broad explanation of the topic of the thesis and a "road ahead" that will assist the reader by mapping out what this topic will cover, why it needs to be covered and what contributions can be made by doing this thesis. From the outset, a context must be established in order to understand what terrorism is and how it particularly affects Africa, in particular the West African nations of LCS. Why should the world care about the prospects of terrorism in West Africa? This thesis will answer that question and show through case studies that indeed terrorism is rampant here and that the US must act accordingly.

Chapter 2: Literature Review

An overview of the sources that were used during the discovery of this topic. Books, articles, magazines and Internet web sites were used to collect, educate and structure this thesis. The centerpiece article is by Nicolas Sambanis who uses the Collier-Hoeffler (CH) model developed by the World Bank in 2000. This model has been extremely helpful in determining research relating to conflict and development.

Chapter 3: Research Methodology

By following an analytical and inductive approach, I will look at the occurrence of terrorism in West Africa through specific observations and pattern analysis followed by a predicted explanation, conclusions and recommendations. By using pair wise comparisons modeled and explain in Sambanis' use of the World Bank CH model for three countries against a myriad of weighted criteria I will show the relationship between these countries and the prospects of terrorism as they relate to those criteria. I will explain why the criteria were chosen and why they are weighted as they are. This chapter will be closely linked to the Sambanis research and the importance of criteria like economics and education.

Chapter 4: Analysis

By explaining the comparison charts in chapter three, analysis must then occur as to why the selected criteria were weighted against a particular country. Each country will garner different outcomes (scores) per each criteria and it is these different scores that will lead to a discussion and analysis of why these occurred. Sambanis has already chosen these criteria but other criteria will be considered and a discussion as to why or why not they might be used will occur. This chapter will fill in these comparisons by using the pair-wise method, as seen in the CH model. As this occurs conclusions will begin to form based upon analysis of these comparisons. Political violence against noncombatants will be discussed here and how this is important in determining the extent of terrorism in these countries. Interestingly, each of the three countries chosen for this study has had different colonial influences. Liberia, arguably, came from American roots, Cotê d'Ivoire was French and Sierra Leone was British.

Chapter 5: Child Soldiers

This chapter shows how child soldiers violates the fundamental rights of children, exploits youth for political purposes, subjects them to slaughter and the ravages of war, and immerses them in a system that sanctions killing. It also poses formidable security risks for others. A society that mobilizes and trains its young for war weaves violence into the fabric of life, increasing the likelihood that violence and war will be its future. Children who have been robbed of education and taught to kill often contribute to further militarization, lawlessness, and violence. The problem is especially severe in developing countries, in which children constitute nearly half the population and in which children are often reared in a system that mixes war, poverty, violence, hunger, environmental degradation, and political instability. The variables will have been looked at in chapter 4.

Chapter 6: Conclusion

This final chapter reviews the conclusions made in chapter four, answers the key questions of the thesis, summarizes West Africa's current state of affairs with respect to political violence and US foreign policy, and concludes with recommendations for which country, in particular, should be the focus of US foreign policy as it relates to hegding political violence against noncombatants and economic assistance. The question of, "Is there anything the US can do about what was discussed in chapter four?" will be discussed here. Questions like, "How will the US respond to terrorism in West Africa?"

and, "What are the policy US implications of the outcomes of the comparisons in chapter four?" are questions that will also be examined.

CHAPTER 2

LITERATURE REVIEW

Introduction

There is no shortage of literature on the topic of terrorism. The following

literature review is intended to set the stage for the analysis by giving the reader

necessary background on the topic. In writing this literature review, my purpose is to

convey to the reader what knowledge and ideas have been established on this topic, and

what their strengths and weaknesses are. The literature review must be defined by a

guiding concept. It is not just a descriptive list of the material available, or a set of

summaries. I try to look critically at this published work. The fact that something has

been published does not mean the findings are automatically trustworthy. In these cases,

however, I found that these publishings have contributed greatly to this thesis.

A. CENTRAL RESEARCH

I. Terrorism or Insurgency?

Merari's "Terrorism as a Strategy of Insurgency"

Areil Merari examines how insurgency and terrorism are linked. In fact, one is a

subset of the other. In many countries in West Africa, civil war vis-à-vis insurgencies

have been repeated many times over. Economics and ethnicity often contribute to this

unrest and it is because of these that often, the author argues, that people do not have a

choice and insurgents consistently use a variety of strategies in their struggle. Terrorism,

he professes, is the easiest form of terrorism and practically always used in an

insurgency. Terrorism does not attempt to challenge government forces directly, but acts

to change perceptions as to the effectiveness or legitimacy of the government itself. This is done by ensuring the widest possible knowledge of the acts of terrorist violence among the target audience. Rarely will terrorists attempt to "control" terrain, as it ties them to identifiable locations and reduces their mobility and security. Terrorists as a rule avoid direct confrontations with government forces. A guerilla force may have something to gain from a clash with a government combat force, such as proving that they can effectively challenge the military effectiveness of the government. A terrorist group has nothing to gain from such a clash. This is not to say that they do not target military or security forces, but that they will not engage in anything resembling a "fair fight", or even a "fight" at all. Terrorists use methods that neutralize the strengths of conventional forces. Bombings and mortar attacks on civilian targets where military or security personnel spend off-duty time, ambushes of undefended convoys, and assassinations of poorly protected individuals are common tactics. The ultimate goal of an insurgency is to challenge the existing government for control of all or a portion of its territory, or force political concessions in sharing political power.

Insurgencies require the active or tacit support of some portion of the population involved. External support, recognition or approval from other countries or political entities can be useful to insurgents, but is not required. A terror group does not require and rarely has the active support or even the sympathy of a large fraction of the population. While insurgents will frequently describe themselves as "insurgents" or "guerillas", terrorists will not refer to themselves as "terrorists" but describe themselves using military or political terminology ("freedom fighters", "soldiers", "activists"). Terrorism relies on public impact, and is therefore conscious of the advantage of avoiding the negative connotations of the term "terrorists" in identifying themselves.

14

Table 1. A Basic Classification of Political Violence (Merari)

		TARGET	
		STATE	**CITIZENS**
INITIATOR	**STATE**	Full-scale war; belligerent; activity in peacetime, e.g., cloak-and-dagger operations and punitive strikes.	Law enforcement legal and illegal oppression.
	CITIZENS	Guerrilla; insurgent terrorism; coup d'etat; Leninist revolution	Vigilante terrorism; ethnic terrorism

The Collier-Hoeffler Model

Andrea Bohnstedt of World Markets Research Centre states, "The number of civil conflicts now exceeds that of international military conflicts. Not only have civil wars frightening humanitarian implications, but they also lead to economic decline and a destruction of a country's economic base, as examples from countries like Burundi, Liberia, Sierra Leone and Angola show. In a study for the Centre for the Study of African Economies at the Department of Economics of Oxford University (UK), Paul Collier and Anke Hoeffler attempt a quantitative analysis of civil war to calculate its effects on a national, regional and global level." Collier and Hoeffler (CH) is the central piece of literature upon which this thesis rests. The model they developed is used in Chapter 3 and from that analyses are vetted in Chapter 4. Especially in Africa, political violence, civil war and economic depravity all contribute to terrorism in this focused African region. In this paper the authors apply an econometric model of civil war to the analysis of conflict in sub-Saharan Africa. The research shows that Africa has had a similar incidence of civil conflict to that of other developing regions, and that, with minor exceptions, its conflicts are consistent with the global pattern of behavior. However, the structure of risk differs considerably from other regions. Africa's economic characteristics have made it more vulnerable to conflict, but this has been offset by social characteristics that make its societies atypically safe. The paper analyzes the contrasting trends of conflict: rising in Africa and declining in other regions. Africa's rising trend of conflict is due to its atypically poor economic performance.

The World Bank's project on the economics of civil wars, crime and violence, which is headed by Paul Collier, seeks to determine the following: the economic and political factors that increase the risk of civil war, terrorism, and violent crime; policies that are conducive to reducing these risks; and the socio-economic policy difference between post-conflict societies which have high levels of violence, and those societies without such problems. In terms of civil war, this project has two specific foci. First, to investigate and analyze the economic causes and consequences of civil wars. Second, to study the inter-relationships between economic, political, and social variables as they affect the probability that civil war will occur as well as the duration and intensity of these wars. It is anticipated that these analyses will provide insights that will facilitate the generation of economic policies that will reduce the probability of war and reduce human suffering in post-conflict countries (World Bank Group).

The work of Paul Collier and Anke Hoeffler appear to be amongst the most sophisticated. These scholars use a panel data set of conflict over the period 1960-99 to examine the risk of civil war using logit regressions. The authors employ a set of rational choice models of rebellion that revolve around two contrasting motivations for rebellion, namely "greed" and "grievance". The simple greed-rebellion model holds that rebellion will occur if it is financially profitable provided rebel forces are able to evade, endure or repel assaults by government armed forces. The simple grievance model states that war will occur as a consequence of one or more grievances, such as inter-group hatred, political exclusion, and vengeance. Through an intensive statistical analysis, of the global pattern of large-scale conflict from 1965, Collier and Hoeffler found that the grievance models had low explanatory power, while greed models perform well (Collier, 2000). In fact, in another article Collier claims through statistical analyses that economic agendas appear to be central to the origins of many civil wars (Collier 2000, 91).

The models that Collier and Hoeffler construct and the conclusions they draw are thought provoking and certainly challenge conventional wisdom. They are correct in arguing that the economic dimensions of civil war have been neglected. The political economy of rebel groups is a glaring gap in the literature. However, there are certain weaknesses with Collier's and Hoeffler's grievance model. Inter-ethnic and inter-religious hatreds are over-emphasized, while issues of governance, socio-economic deprivation and security concerns are not adequately accounted for. These omissions, if adequately addressed, could have significant implications for their analysis.

In terms of governance, the state's lack of institutional capacity to manage ordinary political and social conflict is often a fundamental cause of armed conflict in

Africa. That is when states do not have the resources and expertise to resolve disputes and grievances, distribute resources equitably, manage competition and protect the rights of citizens, individuals and groups may resort to violence. Socio-economic conditions, with the exception of income distribution, are not included in the grievance model. According to Nathan, in African countries the risk of violence increases when poor socio-economic conditions suddenly deteriorate even more; when government is corrupt and unresponsive to the needs of its people; and when poverty and unemployment are linked to an inequitable distribution of wealth (Nathan, 2000, 190). Nathan looks at four areas that, if found in a country, will increase violence or at least the threat of violence. These are: authoritarian rule, marginalization of ethnic minorities, socio-economic deprivation combined with inequality, and the inability of states to manage normal political and social conflict effectively. As they are the primary causes of large-scale violence, they need to be at the center of any external intervention plan and to be addressed properly for peace to be sustainable.

"On the Incidence of Civil War in Africa" by Paul Collier and Anke Hoeffler

In their paper Collier and Hoeffler apply an econometric model of civil war to conflict analysis in sub-Saharan Africa. They explain that Africa has had a similar prevalence of civil conflict to that of other developing regions, and that, with slight exceptions, its conflicts are consistent with the global pattern of behavior. Nonetheless, the composition of risk differs considerably from other of the world's regions. Africa's economic distinctiveness has made it more susceptible to conflict, but this has been counterbalanced by social characteristics, which make its societies uncharacteristically safe, i.e., because of its strong tribal and family base, Africa does have local and tribal law that generally allows for a safe environment. They then analyze the different trends

of conflict: rising in Africa and waning in other world regions. They show that the model

predicts these trends. Africa's rising tendency of conflict is due to its atypically meager

economic performance.

Sambanis' "Using Case Studies to Expand the Theory of Civil War"

Chapter three of this thesis is the keystone to why terrorism prospects exist in

West Africa and what are the factors and furthermore, why these factors are linked to

insurgencies and economics. Using the CH model developed for the World Bank by Yale

University is the vehicle by which variables are used to determine what causes a country

(in this case LCS) to have a tendency delve into a civil war/insurgency that then links to

the use of terrorism in these areas. Case studies can assist in building better theoretical

models. The World Bank-Yale University case study project covered twenty countries

and approximately thirty wars. The case studies suggest a number of improvements and

additions to the CH model. Initially, civil war must be defined and measured better. It is

my opinion that many wars are omitted in the CH dataset, whereas other wars are

included for indistinct reasons. Second, some of the hypotheses that are derived from the

CH model—e.g. the hypothesized link between ethnicity or democracy and civil war—

must be refined and clarified so that the model tests clearly defined theoretical

propositions. Third, the optional measures and model specifications suggested by the case

studies imply the need for different estimation methods. Fourth, the cases do suggest that

the assumption of unit homogeneity that underlies the CH model may be challenged on a

number of grounds. In richer nations, the state may be stronger and political institutions

more stable, all factors that can reduce the possibility of civil war. In poorer states, political institutions will be weaker and less able to deal with inter-ethnic conflict. The CH model's predictions seem to be that political variables "do not matter" for civil war.

Sambanis reminds us that the case study project was not designed to test the CH model. Hypothesis testing was done through econometric methods (the application of statistical methods to the study of economic data and problems)(Merriam-Webster), using a large cross-sectional, time-series dataset. The case studies were a secondary line of inquiry designed to illuminate some of the pathways through which independent variables influence the dependent variable and to explore interactions among the independent variables (Sambanis, 2003). A key conclusion of the case studies is that the causal mechanisms that are implicit in the CH analysis are frequently incorrect or poorly understood. In numerous cases, the model correctly predicts an outcome for the wrong reasons; in other cases, the model fails to accurately predict a war because it has not properly specified the core relationships. The case studies have allowed a better appreciation of the conditions by which different variables influence the possibility of civil war.

Sambanis addresses how observers often see greed and grievances as explanations of insurgence. He mentions that greed and grievance are often "shades of the same problem" and "alternative interpretations of the same phenomenon". Indeed, we often see more political greed and economic grievance than the other way around. He summarizes by stating, "If political institutions can reduce grievances and if economic variables influence the stability of political institutions, then economic variables indirectly affect 'grievance' factors in the CH model. And if state failure or government illegitimacy turns domestic politics into a near-anarchic world, then what CH call 'greed' is really synonymous to the pursuit of survival. Civil war [perpetuated by terrorism] may be a response to either 'greed' or 'grievance' but most often they will be the result of both. We must now move beyond the greed-grievance distinction to explain why some countries are more prone to civil war than others" (Sambanis, 2003).

II. Violence Against Noncombatants

Child Soldiers

Most child soldiers are aged between 14 and 18. While many enlist "voluntarily" research shows that such adolescents see few alternatives to involvement in armed conflict. Some enlist as a means of survival in war-torn regions after family, social and economic structures collapse or after seeing family members tortured or killed by government forces or armed groups. Others join up because of poverty and lack of work or educational opportunities. Many girls have reported enlisting to escape domestic servitude, violence and sexual abuse (Child-soldiers.org). The Convention on the Rights of the Child treaty spells out the basic human rights that children everywhere - without discrimination - have: the right to survival; to develop to the fullest; to protection from harmful influences, abuse and exploitation; to participate fully in family, cultural and social life. The International Labor Organization (ILO) has published several conventions and the International Criminal Court in Rome, Italy has enforced these. This organization has been one of the proponents of anti-child labor movements, to include those acts that force or persuade children to be in the employ or service or armies or militias. For instance, the ILO Worst Forms of Child Labor Convention 182: This convention was adopted on 16 June 1999 and came into force on 19 November 2000. It commits each state, which ratifies it to "take immediate and effective measures to secure the prohibition

21

and elimination of the worst forms of child labor as a matter of urgency". The term "child" applies to all persons under the age of 18 years and the worst forms of child labor include: all forms of slavery or practices similar to slavery, such as the sale and trafficking of children, debt bondage and serfdom and forced or compulsory labor, including forced or compulsory recruitment of children for use in armed conflict (Article 3a)(ILO.org). Many children join armed groups because of economic or social pressure, or because children believe that the group will offer food or security. Others are forcibly recruited, "press-ganged" or abducted by armed groups. Interestingly, there also seems to be a link between traditional religious beliefs and the induction of child soldiers into armies and militias. Certainly, economics plays a major role in why civil wars occur, nonetheless, economics also forces these children to make critical decisions and often these children are pushed into service because of the strong traditional religious beliefs they have. Holy men or shamans (witch doctors) often hold great sway over local crowds. Children being very impressionable rarely make the distinction between rational and irrational choices; especially when those decisions may mean, it could be perceived, a better life because they are "fighting" for a cause and often are guaranteed meals and adventure.

B. STRENGTHS AND WEAKNESSES OF THE LITERATURE

This section discusses the relative strengths and weaknesses of the literature on terrorism/insurgency and economic agendas. A new trend has emerged in the relationship between terrorism/insurgency and economics. This trend has two dimensions, namely that valuable resources have been used to finance civil wars, and that the perpetuation of war in certain African countries is perceived to be an alternative way of generating profits. Most academics, researchers and journalists without any detailed analysis of the political economies of rebel movements and insurgents have accepted the first dimension.

Most of the literature is concerned with describing and/or analyzing the second dimension. The popular assumption is that economic greed is a significant, if not the predominant, driving force in many of the current conflicts in Africa. To wit, there are a number of publications that provide unequivocal statements that a direct link exists between the desire to acquire economic wealth by elites and civil war. However, in general, this assumption remains untested.

The media has had a major influence on this state of affairs. Since 1998 numerous media articles have emerged that have described in some detail the role economic agendas play in African wars/insurgencies/terrorist hotbeds. The most common subject matter has been on how greed and the illicit trade in diamonds continue to fuel violent conflicts in Angola, Sierra Leone and the DRC. Many international newspapers have carried such stories, with lengthy articles having appeared in the *New York Times* and *the Mail and Guardian* (an African online newspaper), to name but a few. Many of these media reports were inspired by the release of publications by Global Witness, the United Nations Panel of Experts, Human Rights Watch and Partnership Africa Canada.

In terms of the academic literature a distinction can be made between theoretical and empirical work. Publications of a theoretical nature generally deal with the conceptualization of the relationship between terrorism/insurgency and economic agendas, and how insurgent economies interact with the global economy. Examples include publications by civil war researcher David Keen. Keen demonstrates that war is not always fought for an ultimate victory or political advances and does not simply reflect a breakdown of society. War might instead represent an alternative system of profit, power, and protection. Violence pays economic dividends that war can amplify by conferring both means and legitimacy on predatory winners. Examining the empirical pattern of civil wars between 1965 and 1999, Collier furthers Keen's argument, asserting "the true cause of much civil war is not the loud discourse of grievance but the silent force of greed." In his essay "Doing Well out of War," Collier finds no explanatory power in what he identifies as the main elements of grievances, which include inequality, government incompetence, repression, and ethnic fractionalization (these are variables within his model); in fact, the latter two reduce the risk of conflict. In contrast, greed is closely correlated with the occurrence of civil war.

> Now, in the case of Sierra Leone, this is a different kind of terrorism, but definitely the use of terror against civilians, I think that the RUF, the rebels there, they have systematically used terror in pursuit of power and wealth, but what strikes me most forcibly is that this has actually proven useful for a whole range of groups in Sierra Leone to be able to point to the RUF as the source of evil in the country, and meanwhile pursuing a variety of political and economic ends, including the suppression of democracy, under the cover of war—David Keen.

However, clarity is lacking in terms of what actually constitutes an economic agenda and what does not. In addition, the entire nature of the relationship between terrorism/insurgencies and economic agendas still needs to be explored. Hence this concept and its various dimensions need to be rigorously cross-examined.

To date, no comprehensive empirical study of the dynamics of insurgent economies and the mechanisms of greed in the context of armed conflict in the post-Cold War era has been conducted. Not even the case study research of rebel movements provides insight into this area. Generally, only brief descriptions of the political economy of rebel movements are provided, with anecdotal references being frequently used.

24

In the theoretical literature only econometric analyses are relatively well developed. These analyses involve the application of mathematical and statistical techniques to study problems, analyze data, and develop and test theories and models. It has been possible for econometric analyses and models to be generated, as no extensive field research is required, with the exception of securing a reliable data set. However, econometric analyses are constrained by the fact that data originating from conflict hotspots is often unavailable, and where available it tends to be unreliable. Case in point; Sambanis omits data on Liberia due to the intense fighting and depredated infrastructure. This case study certainly is relevant to the literature pool but the omission of it, I opine, was because of it being a hotspot.

The econometric models, however, have some serious deficiencies. In the case of the greed and grievance models devised by Collier and Hoeffler three shortcomings can be identified. First, Collier and Hoeffler claim to compare two contrasting motivations for rebellion, namely greed and grievance. However, while the grievance model considers motivations for armed conflict, such as inter-ethnic hatreds, the greed model appears to focus on opportunities for rebellion (e.g. size of the rebel movement, relative military advantage and cost of recruitment), rather than motivations. Second, the grievance model does not reflect the myriad of sophisticated theories of the causes of armed conflict. Third, as the models are concerned with major trends, and hence indigenous/unique features are not included in the models.

The policy-oriented literature is also still in its early stages of development, however, the sanctions, human rights and private security literatures provide some well constructed policy proposals. These proposals include detailed technical recommendations for the improvement of sanctions regimes, increased respect for human rights, the reformation of the diamond and oil industries, and the regulation of the private security companies.

Despite the fact that many African scholars, such as First, Hutchful, Mazrui and Mamdani, have studied and theorized about armed conflict in Africa, the literature on war and economic agendas in Africa is dominated by academics from Europe and the United States.

> The blood of the innocent cries out not just for a coalition against terrorism but for a coalition in search of genuine peace. I grew up in a Kenya engulfed in a war of liberation which the British called "terrorist" -- the Mau Mau war of the 1950s. I have personally met people like Nelson Mandela and Yassir Arafat, men once denounced as terrorists, but who lived to win the Nobel Prize for Peace. Some of their acts of war were in the past localized and regional. But now it is not just terrorists "who can run but cannot hide." Such a situation has become the human condition itself—Dr. Ali Mazrui.

There are two possible reasons for the absence of an African voice. First, the sub-field of war and economic agendas is new and is being studied by only a handful of scholars. Should it grow in popularity, then it is simply a matter of time before African academics make contributions. Second, African scholars, by virtue of their physical location, are more in touch with the complex nature of civil wars/terrorism/insurgencies on the continent, and consequently do not enthusiastically subscribe to the greed thesis.

The literature set that I discovered does have some positive qualities. Its greatest strength is that it accentuates the economic dimension of violent conflict, in particular the role and impact that the availability of valuable primary resources has on terrorism/insurgency. I must emphasize that these primary resources need to be taken into account in order to have any hope of securing a sustainable peace agreement. This literature set is multidisciplinary in nature and is characterized by a number of creative

approaches to the relationship between terrorism/insurgency and economic agendas.

CHAPTER 3

RESEARCH METHODOLOGY

Introduction

This chapter outlines the use of pair wise comparison and explains the criteria used in the comparing the countries of Liberia, Cotê d'Ivoire and Sierra Leone. Nicholas Sambanis explains, "More than one hundred forty civil wars around the world since 1945 have killed approximately 20 million people and displaced 67 million." He goes to say that civil wars occur disproportionately in poor countries and retard economic development in entire regions. The countries of LCS all fall within the category of poorest countries in the world, according to the United Nations Conference on Trade and Development (UNCTAD). By using comparative case structures of the LCS countries the internal political and economic problems can be examined and the tendency for that country to experience political violence can be observed.

On examining these countries, the question must be asked: "Why does/has civil war occurred here? By examining the case studies this question should be answered because the independent variable is repeatedly linked to the dependent variables showing the reasons for civil war. Subsequently, it must also be asked: "Is there political violence, and if so, does it occur against noncombatants. It is this link between the occurrence of civil war and the occurrence of political violence against noncombatants that will show that there are indeed factors that result in political violence and terrorism against noncombatants in these countries in West Africa.

By definition, civil war involves its citizens and is waged, in part, by civilians. The civilian force is often under equipped and is lacks state funding and organization. For this reason the civilian force must resort to any means necessary to even the proverbial playing field. Recruitment often nets to those that are easily persuaded and have little to lose. Ideology usually comes in the form of hysteria, groupthink, substance abuse, traditional religious views interwoven with mainstream religion and fatalism. To whom does this seem to appeal the most? The children easily fall prey to these.

Goals and Explanation of Criteria

The main purpose for using case studies in this chapter (the LCS countries) is to enhance the quantitative analysis of the CH model so as to progress implications that can be drawn as they relate to the selected criteria and the prospects of terrorism. Sambanis proposes, "Is the research design in each case study determinate? Do the studies suffer from selection bias? Can the cases say anything about the phases of civil war, except the onset?" It is precisely these questions that will lead me to draw conclusions that, it is hoped, will show that political violence (brought about by the onset of civil war/insurgencies) in fact does constitute terrorism. The case studies make several contributions. They help us identify several causal mechanisms through which independent variables in economic models influence the dependent variable –i.e. the risk of civil war/political violence onset. It is at this juncture that I must add another dependent variable to this study that Sambanis does not entirely cover. Civil war, through the study of these independent variables, will become evident as to how the likelihood of its occurrence. However, political violence must also be examined in these case studies as a product of culture and the presence of child soldiers. Furthermore, political violence against noncombatants must also be looked at in these case studies. Civil war may not necessarily occur in a country based on the reasons linked to the independent variables but if political violence, linked to the presence of child soldiers can be established then it can be shown that civil war is an absolute catalyst for political violence against noncombatants. Chapter 5 will look more in depth at the cause of child soldiers and why they exist and to what extent they propagate political violence against noncombatants.

By examining the independent variables one can begin to see how one country may have a higher propensity for political violence than another compared country. Once the link has been made between economic, political and social factors as to the likelihood of political violence, conclusions and inferences can then be made as to why an insurgency or political movement may choose terrorism to further its goals. Sambanis does admit, however, that the CH model of war commencement is accurate for some of the cases he looks at (161 in total) but it frequently comes up short as to describing the process through which civil war/political violence occurs. I have chosen the three case studies for this study because of the high incidence, historically, of political violence and to then use Sambanis' use of the CH model to predict the occurrence of political violence in the future. Can a political violence process be gleaned from this observation? I am not sure; however, because certain independent variables exist and have always existed in these countries, the likelihood of continued political violence in these countries is high. I am not hypothesizing that these countries will never break free from the bounds of political violence as we see it in its present form, but due to the presence of some of these independent variables these countries certainly will see political violence again. Chapter 5 will link the affects child soldiers have with political violence to noncombatants. Where you find child soldiers, you will find political violence against noncombatants.

Independent Variables

Sambanis uses the following independent variables as varying measures through which incidences of political violence and civil war have a likelihood to occur. Sambanis says this of the CH model:

> According to the CH model, rebellion is sustained through the looting of natural resources, extortion of local population, and support from ethnic Diasporas. Insurgency is less likely when the state is strong or when the economic opportunity costs of rebellion are high. State strength is not well theorized in the model and is approximated by the country's economic strength (GDP per capita). The expectation is that relatively richer states will be bureaucratically more efficient and will have the resources needed to defend themselves against a rebellion. Since insurgency is more likely as the supply of rebel labor increases, strong states can reduce the available labor supply by decreasing the net expected gains from rebellion (by reducing the probability that the rebellion will be successful).

Notice the strong linkages between economics and the propensity for political violence. The most of the independent variables, in some way, could be linked to economics. Keep these following points in mind as the case studies are examined: poverty exacerbates the risk of civil war, high economic growth reduces the risk of political violence (allegedly because the opportunity costs of violence rise—i.e. the more economically secure an individual is the more he has to loose by engaging in political violence and therefore must decide whether to continue to fight or not based upon what he thinks he might gain or loose from that decision—and the technology of insurgency (mountainous terrain, external financing from Diasporas) increases the risk of war by making it more viable. Additionally, secondary school enrollment, especially in males, has been shown to decrease the risk of political violence (Sambanis, 2003, 12).

31

Economic variables: GDP, Growth, Education

Weak economic indicators, the CH model strongly predicts, is what really predicts a civil war or political violence and not necessarily political repression. The LCS countries in the preceding years to civil war had a declining per capita income, low education levels and waning growth. In Sierra Leone, real per capita income was just over $900 before the war commenced down from $1,400 in the 1970s (Sambanis, 2003, 19). Looking at the CH model broadly, lack of education can be particularly obvious as a variable for the onset of war, especially in Africa. The CH model however, lacks *how* education contributed to political violence risk.

Economic growth is very easily tracked in the CH as to indication of the possibility of political violence. In Sierra Leone, economic growth was negative before the start of the war in 1991 (Sambanis, 2003). According to Sambanis, in the couple years preceding war in a country, low-level violence (with roots in political violence) reduces both income and growth. It seems to be self-perpetuating. Prior to war, economic growth declines but during the declining years low-level crime strips away the ability for a country to possibly recover and prevent the nose dive toward political violence. Because of the negative impact civil war and political violence has on a country, Sambanis says that this in itself hampers economic recovery and may lead to a higher incidence of that country falling into war again. In other cited cases by Sambanis he states that there might even be cause for political violence due to *increased* economic growth, but in the case of the LCS countries I disagree with this. Due to the extreme poverty that exists there economic growth would surely effect stabilization and assist in civil war deterrence.

GDP is a measure of the state's economic strength. As political violence ensues or as terrorism occurs in a country, its ability to respond and handle the situation has a lot to do with its capacity to respond. Resources like weapons, well trained police forces/gendarmeries and higher opportunity costs play an important role in the ability for a state to deal with civil strife. Linked to the GDP though is the authority a state has over the country. For example, Kenya has a relatively low GDP but an authoritarian state and their incidence of civil war has been low. In the cases of the LCS countries, we do not see either a strong state or strong GDP and therefore civil war and political violence has been prevalent there.

Natural resources are central to this discussion. Resource predation, Sambanis explains about the CH model, may have several problems with the premise that looting as a motive for rebellion and looting as a means to sustain rebellion (Sambanis, 2003). If a country has enough natural resources as a whole, the CH model will not predict that political violence will occur in the less rich regions of a country. The country must be looked at as a whole. In most cases, argues Sambanis, looting is a mechanism used to sustain rebellion and political violence and it is not necessarily a motive for political violence. In nearby countries like Nigeria and Cameroon, oil has a unique impact on political thought but for the LCS countries this will not be discussed.

Population

Population has a very significant affect on the occurrence of civil war. Theoretically, the CH model outlines, is that the larger the population the easier it should be to find a group to challenge the state. It must be noted that often, as a whole, an African country might possess a large population, however, upon closer inspection, the state is actually a conglomeration of tribal, ethnic and religious diversity. Thus, as is often the case, a country will be split up along those boundaries thereby decreasing the *size* of the country into fractional areas. This may reduce the risk of political violence. Not only does "how many" play a key role here but also "where are they" is vital. Urbanization, which is linked to GDP, has an impact on war risk. The fact that most political violence does not occur in urban areas suggests that as important as how many people populate a country is what the density of the population is especially around urban centers. Africa's violence tends however, to occur more often in urban areas compared to other states.

Diasporas

This is an interesting variable. The CH model specifically deals with how many of the affected countries nationals residing in the U.S. as the variable her. The larger the Diaspora, the greater the amount of assistance to the rebel group or political violence group and the greater the risk of war (Sambanis, 2003). Important to note that Sambanis expands this term to not just limit those that are residing in the U.S. but also to ethnic groups that may be refugees in cross border communities. Diasporas often support transnational influence of political violence.

Ethnicity and Social Fragmentation, and Polarization

The CH model shows that ethnic diversity does not increase the incidence of civil war. Social fractionalization actually impedes rebellion, states Sambanis. The CH model goes on to show that ethnic dominance raises the risk of political violence. This works when the minority thinks that it is going to be politically dominated and permanently excluded from the running of the state and therefore their well being (Sambanis, 2003).

Ethnic dominance occurred in Cotê d'Ivoire but strong political dominance avoided war. Strong intervening governments were key here to avoid ethnic misgivings. Strong political institutions must be in place in order to assist with ethnic clashes and Sambanis suggests that democracy may be one of these institutions.

Political Institutions

The CH model states that political grievance—moderated by political institutions—do not matter, and consequently does not reduce the possibility of political violence. Sambanis says that this is somewhat contrary to other literature that says that political institutions have positive effects. Sambanis argues that the CH model actually is quite accurate in proving that "does not matter" but needs some qualifying in some of the case studies. In the LCS countries I will show that democracy does matter.

Conclusion

Case studies give us historical and political context for the periods in between periods of civil war n various countries (Sambanis, 2003). This chapter outlined the views of Sambanis and the CH model and the variable against which predictions and analyses will occur with the three countries of LCS. Perhaps missing in these variables is the leadership. Strong political institutions were mentioned but how are these institutions strong? Through force? By ethnic majority? Or does solid leadership play a role—free of corruption and a focus on future prosperity and economic and political freedoms? The CH model is the conventional wisdom and Sambanis does a good job of using the CH model to hang his insights but also offers alternate reasons why a state may have a propensity, or not, to plunge into political violence and civil war.

The CH model, as Sambanis has shown, is not complete with its criteria to predict political violence. Chapter 4 will use the variables explained in this chapter and look at how the countries of LCS may or may not, based on history, seem to moving in a particular direction—toward political violence or away from it.

CHAPTER 4

WEST AFRICAN POLITICAL VIOLENCE ANALYSIS

Introduction

This chapter will use the variables explained in the previous chapter and using the CH model illustrate if the countries of LCS have a propensity to spiral into political violence. This data, except Liberia, comes from the Sambanis work on civil war. At the end of each table I will explain why the variables were marked as shown. Sambanis writes, "The CH model is falsifiable as it generates predictions that, if proven wrong, would invalidate the theory; and the theory clearly identifies the assumptions and variables on which it rests." For Liberia, the table was completed based on personal experience and regional expertise.

A. CASE STUDIES OF LIBERIA, CÔTE D'IVOIRE AND SIERRA LEONE

Liberia

Table 2.   CH Model Applied to Liberia

CH Variable	Association with war onset in CH model	Values of variable	Are variable values consistent with War or no war for relevant period?	Refinements or revisions of the theory with respect to this variable
Primary commodity exports/GDP	Positive	Avg primary commodity exports /GDP Primary commodity exports/GDP for 1959-99 higher than non-war and war countries	Consistent	Liberia has never turned its dependence on primary commodity exports into an asset. It imports more than it exports.
GDP per capita	Negative	Consistently lower than non-war countries and close to war countries.	Consistent	Credible redistribution from post-war efforts increased opportunity cost of rebel labor, hence decreased the conflict risk of low GDP/capita. Cuts in public sector

GDP per capita (cont'd)				wages and civil service downsizing deepened poverty and violence did break out in 2003, suggesting that cuts in redistribution exacerbate the problem.
Diaspora	Positive	Because of close connection with the U.S.	Inconsistent	Support for change has been strong and has had resonance. Educated and with financial means, Liberians abroad, especially in the US, have been politically influential.
GDP Growth	Negative	Negative growth in some years mostly lower than the war country avg. High growth in other years; much higher growth than non-war country avg.	Mixed	Contributing to West Africa's relatively slow growth was the decline in Nigeria's real GDP growth from 10.2 % in 2003 to 4.6 % in 2004. Also contributing to the weak performance in West Africa was the ongoing political crisis in Côte d'Ivoire, which led to yet another year of slow real GDP growth.
Mountainous terrain	Positive	Very few mountains.	Consistent	
Geographic dispersion	Positive	Lower than in both war and non-war countries.	Consistent	
Social Fractionalization	Negative	Likely to be moderate given high ethnic fractionalization and low religious fractionalization	Unclear	Social polarization may be more significant.
Population size	Positive	Higher than the mean.	Inconsistent	War and threat of war have played a large part in population displacement to neighboring states and to its capital city thus population size fluctuates greatly.
Ethnic fractionalization	Negative, but non-significant	High ethnic fractionalization relative to war and non-war countries. Albeit there are more than 18 ethnic groups, natural groupings divide the population into 3-4 ethnic groupings at most.	Consistent by the CH measure, inconsistent by case study's measure. (Not significant in CH).	Measure of ethnic fractionalization should account for natural groupings of ethnic groups.
Religious fractionalization	Non-significant			

Ethnic dominance	Positive	No ethnic dominance according to CH; however, the two largest groups (Americo-Liberians and the Mandingo) have swapped power many times and the political seems to revolve around these two groups	Consistent with CH measure, but inconsistent by case study's measure.	A more accurate measure would reflect political dominance. Such dominance can be mitigated by a credible (i.e. with assurance that it will continue in the future) redistribution strategy that assigns some powerful positions to members of other groups.
Income inequality	Non-significant	Same level of income inequality as war and non-war countries. Capital city dwellers are richer than rural dwellers.	Consistent	
Democracy	Positive	Because of the close ties with the US, Liberians know and understand democracy and the benefits thereof. All political institutions and processes are modeled after US.	Consistent	They know they want democracy but cannot seem to sustain it. A free and economically stable state mitigates the need/desire to engage in war. The irony is that Liberia was established based upon the tenants of freedom from slavery.
Peace duration	Negative	Since 1989, Liberia has been in several civil wars.	Inconsistent	

Five years after UNAMSIL began, Sierra Leone is the poorest country on earth—except, perhaps, for Liberia, which does not even have data. The situation is on shaky ground, and new thinking is needed. One way to approach the problem is simply to ask about the incentives and the means at the disposal of those things that spoil the way ahead. The incentives have been and continue to be economic pillage. The means have been violence during wartime and the creation of parallel systems of hierarchy and benefaction during peacetime.

Peacekeeping operations more or less effectively diminish the belligerents' fighting capacities but they have done little to put the spoils of the state beyond reach. After investing billions of dollars, the international community has the right to expect more. Roads in both countries are close to impassable. Liberia has no electrical, sewage, or landline telephone systems. Education and health services in Liberia are minimal, rule of law is inadequate. After fourteen years respectively of on-and-off warfare, Liberian citizens certainly have the right to ask more. Long-term security guarantees, such as Sierra Leone has, should be the first step in a more promising process.

<u>Côte d'Ivoire</u>

Table 3.   CH Model Applied to Côte d'Ivoire

CH Variable	Association with war onset in CH model	Values of variable Period 1: 1960-1993 Period 2: 1994-1999	Are variable values consistent with War or no war for relevant period?	Refinements or revisions of the theory with respect to this variable
Primary commodity exports/GDP	Positive or inverted	P1: Avg primary commodity exports /GDP P2: Primary commodity exports/GDP for 1959-99 higher than non-war and war countries	P1 and P2: Inconsistent	P1: Cotê d'Ivoire turned its dependence on primary commodity exports into an asset.
GDP per capita	Negative	P1: Consistently lower than non-war countries & close to war countries. P2: Low compared to war and non-war P1 and P2: GDP/capita in the south higher than avg, but lower in the north.	P1 and P2: Inconsistent	P1: Credible redistribution increases opportunity cost of rebvel labor, hence decreases the conflict risk of low GDP/capita. P2: Cuts in public sector wages & civil service downsizing deepened poverty and violence did break out in 2000, suggesting that cuts in redistribution exacerbate the problem.
Diaspora	Positive	No mention of a Diaspora	N/a	
GDP Growth	Negative	P1: Negative growth in some years mostly lower than the war	P1: Mixed P2: Consistent	Despite the resumption of high growth rate in 1994 after devastation

		country avg. High growth in other years; much higher growth than non-war country avg. P2: High growth		of CFA Franc, poverty deepened among all ethnic groups due to massive fall in public sector wages and downsizing of civil service. Hence a better measure of economic conditions may be data from household surveys.
Mountainous terrain	Positive	Very few mountains.	P1 and P2: Consistent	
Geographic dispersion	Positive	Lower than in both war and non-war countries.	P1 and P2: Consistent	
Social fractionalization	Negative	CH data not available; likely to be moderate given high ethnic fractional-ization & low religious fractional-ization	P1 and P2: Unclear	Social polarization may be more significant.
Population size	Positive	P1: Avg higher than mean. P2: Higher than the mean.	P1 and P2: Inconsistent	
Ethnic Fractionalization	Negative, but non-significant	P1 and P2: High ethnic fractionalization relative to war & non-war countries. Albeit there are more than 70 ethnic groups, natural groupings divide the population into 3-4 ethnic groupings at most.	P1 and P2: Consistent by the CH measure, inconsistent by case study's measure. (Not significant in CH).	Measure of ethnic fractionalization should account for natural groupings of ethnic groups.
Religious Fractionalization	Non-significant	P1 and P2: Low religious fractional-ization relative to war and non-war countries. But there is a strong cleavage between the Muslim north and the Christian and animist south.	P1 and P2: Consistent. (Not significant in CH)	Religious polarization may be more significant, especially if ranked with ethnic, regional and economic cleavages; argued to be the most divisive of these cleavages in Cotê d'Ivoire.
Ethnic dominance	Positive	P1 and P2: No ethnic dominance according to CH; largest ethnic group is 23% of the population. But the Akan regional group (41.4% of population) dominated political center from independence, through dominance	P1 and P2: Consistent by CH measure, but inconsistent by case study's measure.	A more accurate measure would reflect political dominance, possibly held by an ethno-regional group less than 45% of the population. Such dominance can be mitigated by a credible (i.e. with assurance that it will continue in the future) redistribution

		was challenged by emergence of ethno-regional parties beginning in 1990.		strategy that assigns some powerful positions to members of other groups.
Income inequality	Non-significant	P1 and P2: Same level of income inequality as war and non-war countries. But southerners are richer than northerners.	P1 and P2: Consistent	
Democracy Democracy (cont'd)	Non-significant	P1 and P2: Non-democratic regime. Regime liberalized to include multiple parties in 1990. 1994 law required voters & candidates & their parents to have been born in Côte d'Ivoire.	P1 and P2: Consistent (Not significant in CH)	
Peace duration	Negative	P1 and P2: There were no civil wars in Côte d'Ivoire through 1999.	P1 and P2: Consistent	

Non-CH Variables of possible interest for Civil War Onset/Avoidance (Sambanis)

– *Credible redistribution.* Through redistribution, the richer southerners (Ivorians) were able to avoid political violence and rebellion from the poorer northerners most of the time, or kept any violence within acceptable bounds if violence occurred. In this way, Côte d'Ivoire was able to avoid civil war, despite possessing several high risk factors. Key aspects of this strategy during period 1 included: large-scale public investment in the poorer region, raising representatives from different ethnic groups to powerful political positions, establishing education as the key to getting lucrative positions, and high wages to public sector employees. In order to be conflict preventing, redistribution must be credible, i.e. it must give believable assurances that it will continue in the future.

– Colonial policy. A main reason why the Akan have been politically dominant is that the French entered Côte d'Ivoire from the southeast, which is a region where the Akan live and so they were the first to benefit from formal schooling. Also, the capital city of Côte d'Ivoire under French rule was in the southeast. This suggests that a mechanism by which ethno-political dominance can emerge is favoritism, either deliberate or by chance, in colonial policy.

– Social polarization (ranked ethnic, regional, religious and economic polarization). The north-south divide, augmented by ranked economic and religious cleavages, is argued to have dominated the political landscape in Côte d'Ivoire and to have been the key source of potential conflict, i.e. a rebellion of the poorer northerners against the richer and politically dominant southerners.

Sierra Leone

Table 4.   CH Model Applied to Sierra Leone

CH Variable	Association with war onset in CH model	Values of variable Sierra Leone 1991-96	Are variable values consistent with War or no war for relevant period?	Refinements or revisions of the theory with respect to this variable
Primary commodity exports/GDP	Positive or inverted-U	Primary commodity exports/GDP (0.074) lower than both no-war countries (0.169) & civil war countries (0.149). CH underestimate diamond exports due to predominantly illicit nature of industry. In 1970s before formal diamond industry collapsed, diamonds were 50% of official exports & production hasn't declined.	Consistent	Illicit diamond industry thrived also prior to the conflict, often with government involvement & facilitated by the alluvial & widely dispersed nature of the diamonds. Rebel recruitment base consisted largely of illicit diamond diggers, suggesting a link between a high level of crime involving natural resource extraction and civil war onset.
GDP per capita	Negative	Low GDP per capita (901 in 1990-95),	Consistent	Rather than use GDP per capita to measure

		compared to civil war countries (1645) & especially to non-civil countries 4219).		poverty, use more targeted measures: over 80% of population lived on less than $1/day & country ranked bottom on UNDP Human Development Index for 1991. Unemployment is also a good predictor.
Diaspora	Positive	No mention of a Diaspora	Unknown	
GDP Growth	Negative	Negative GDP growth 1980-89, which is consistent other civil war countries.	Consistent	
Mountainous terrain	Positive	Very few mountains (1.7% of area). No kind of terrain is mentioned by the case study to have been significant.	Inconsistent	
Geographic dispersion	Positive	Lower than in both war & non-war countries.	Inconsistent	
Social fractionalization	Negative	Data not available, but likely to be high given high ethnic fractionalization and moderate religious fractionalization.	Inconsistent	
Population size	Positive	Slightly lower than the mean.	Inconsistent	
Ethnic Fractionalization	Negative, but non-significant	High degree of ethnic fractionalization relative to civil and non-civil war countries.	Inconsistent (Not significant in CH)	
Religious fractionalization	Nonsignificant	Slightly lower degree of religious fractionalization relative to civil and non-civil war countries.	Consistent (Not significant in CH)	
Ethnic dominance	Positive	No ethnic dominance; largest ethnic group corresponds to 30% of the population.	Inconsistent	Measure should include regional political dominance. The ruling All People's Congress was dominated by Northerners & the rebellion started in the Southeast.
Income inequality	Non-significant	Low income inequality relative to civil and non-civil war countries.	Not significant in CH	
Democracy	Non-significant	Non-democratic regime.	Consistent (Not signif't in CH)	

| Peace duration | Negative | There were no civil wars in Sierra Leone from independence to the beginning of the present conflict. | Inconsistent | Include peace duration from conflicts causing less than 1,000 deaths: e.g. the Ndorgbowusu rebellion of 1982 affected the onset of war as would a previous war, i.e. eased rebel recruitment, especially since the rebellion had been brutally suppressed, which increased the incentive to overthrow the government. |

Non-CH Variables of possible interest for Civil War Onset (Sambanis)

- *Historical urban bias in economic policy.* Rural marginalization increased the risk of civil war through three main mechanisms: (1) induced migration to towns and diamond-mining areas, which increased unemployment in those areas and expanded the pool of potential rebels; (2) provided a grievance-based justification for the rebellion and thus facilitated recruitment; and (3) corresponded to a weak state presence in rural areas.

- *Regional marginalization.* Despite providing much of the national wealth, the southeastern regions where the war started were marginalized by the northern based

All People's Congress and this induced many people to join the rebellion.

- *Level of crime prior to the conflict.* This variable has already been discussed in the table as it is related to CH's primary commodity exports/GDP variable. To repeat, an illicit diamond industry thrived also prior to the conflict, at times with government involvement. Rebel recruitment base consisted largely of illicit diamond diggers, suggesting a link between a high level of crime involving natural resource extraction and civil war onset. The growth and sustenance of such crime can be attributed to four main

45

factors: informal economy, high unemployment, distortionary economic policy and illicit diamond trade:

- *Informalization of the economy.* In the 1967 elections, opposition leader Siaka Stevens of the All People's Congress promised illicit miners support if he got their votes. The corporate Sierra Leone Selection Trust was nationalized, but crippled by the late 1970s by state-sponsored looting of its diamond resources through theft, illicit mining and political sabotage.

- *Unemployment* is widespread among diamond diggers, which made them easy recruits for criminal extortion activities. (See also discussion of unemployment below.)

- *Distortionary economic policy.* Exchange and price controls in response to the oil price shocks of the 1970s led to buoyant black markets for foreign currency and essential imports. In neighboring Liberia there were no exchange controls, the US dollar was used as the currency and therefore widely available and diamond export taxes were lower. A lucrative underground trade emerged involving smuggling diamonds often through Liberia to purchase scarce essential imports whose sales in black markets financed purchases of diamonds for further smuggling.

- *Factors which aid the trade in conflict and illicit diamonds:* difficulty in determining a diamond's country of origin, tacit or explicit complicity of transit countries which "re-export" diamonds, and the secretive nature of the diamond industry for security reasons.

- *Human rights abuses* by puppet chiefs led to widespread grievances and to revenge-motivated enlistment in the rebel movement.

- External intervention. Desirous to spread his influence in West African and to install pro-Libyan puppet government, Ghadaffy provided finance and training to the future RUF leader and other Sierra Leonean dissidents. After Charles Taylor launched the Liberian civil war in 1989, he provided a base and some rebels for the RUF to launch the rebellion in March 1991.

- Unemployment. The distortionary economic policy of the 1980s increased unemployment, which most affected youths entering the labor force. Perceiving the corrupt and repressive "system" as the cause of their predicament, these youth became increasingly rebellious—spearheading anti-government agitations, resorting to crime and drugs, and finding inspiration in revolutionary exhortations such as reggae music and Ghadaffy's Green Book—and thus were easy recruits for illicit diamond digging and hence also for the rebellion.

B. SIGNIFICANCE

The causes of civil war are economic oppression of ethnic group(s) by other groups, the self-motivated attempts by ethnic groups to succeed over other groups and low levels of growth. The oppressed will finally revolt, take arms and attempt to obtain a fair share in the economy. The consequences of civil war are increases in defense spending and destruction of infrastructure leading to underdevelopment, a lowering of the quality of life and per capita GDP. The consequences of this are that the oppressed people will get more oppressed, or the oppressed will triumph and oppress the other groups, resulting in more violence in the future. Therefore it seems that the consequences fuel the fires of the future causes. Unless some means other than fighting is found there will be no development and therefore no long-term solution to the problem. The causes of civil conflict lead to the consequences, civil conflict, which will in turn increase the causes. This is the vicious cycle of civil conflict that will inhibit development and growth in many countries in Africa, Asia and in other parts of the world.

Though it is commonly assumed that ethno-linguistic fractionalization is a leading cause behind civil conflict, we find there may be more significant variables contributing to the conflict. Namely: low levels of natural resources, high poverty (low levels of GPD per capita), and lack of strong democratic institutions. The analysis conducted by economists clearly showed that strong institutions have the ability to decrease the probability of incidence of war, for a given level of fractionalization in a society. Additionally, high levels of fractionalization and high levels of homogeneity are negatively related to the possibility of civil conflict, while average levels of fractionalization increase the chances of civil conflict. Though it is difficult to calculate the costs and consequences of a war, it is possible if the necessary data is available.

Furthermore, it is possible that strong government institutions have the ability to stop the oppression and any civil violence associated with it, effectively breaking the cycle. While evidence clearly supports the economic causes as significant causes leading to civil conflict it must be mentioned that there are very passionate and violent emotions that cannot be numerically accounted for in play as well. People's feelings of pride, patriotism and panic are beyond the reach of mere economic influences and play a big role in influencing the final outcome in these struggles.

CHAPTER 5

CHILD SOLDIERS

Introduction

I arrived at the crowded airport late in the afternoon. Passport control seemed nonexistent as people jockeyed for best position to retrieve their bags from the slow moving and squeaky luggage carousel. The physical assault of both the luggage handlers, all vying to carry your bag for any spare change you might have and the pungent, humid air seemed almost too fantastic. As I quickly power-locked the door of the armored Suburban I only then was able to mentally access what it was like to arrive in one of the most meager spots in Africa; Monrovia, Liberia. As the crow flies, the embassy was only 20 miles away but multitudes of roadblocks made for an unhurried journey. It was the children at these roadblocks that caught me in unabashed stares. Children laden with rag-tag clothes, flip-flops made from car tires and dirty faces, at first, made me overlook that they also carried AK-47s. Blood-shot and yellow hued eyes telegraphed that they were on some kind of drug. No smiles at all, not even when I smiled back at them through two inches of Mylared glass. As older soldiers were bossing them around, they seemed hopeless; they seemed distant; they seemed scared; they seemed dangerous. —Mark Patterson.

Children have always been among the most vulnerable civilian casualties of warfare, and older teenagers have often been among those recruited to fight. The new campaign to stop the use of those under 18 as soldiers can be seen as part of the ongoing codification of international humanitarian law, to limit if not entirely stop age-old abuses against human life and dignity.

There is another new reason for the prominence of the issue, vividly seen in recent African conflicts. The availability of light automatic weapons that can be carried even by young children has dramatically increased the usefulness of children in combat. So has the fact that many contemporary conflicts target unarmed civilians rather than pit conventional armies against each other. Armed with an AK-47, even an eight-year-old can go into battle under adult leadership and carry out horrendous slaughter.

Government forces often draft teenagers in the borderline years of 16 to 18, and even 15, as a matter of course. In draft raids, the appearance of being old enough to fight is often enough to justify being dragged along to the recruiting center, sometimes at gunpoint.

Such abuses are most frequent in countries involved in internal conflict. A new report on child soldiers in Africa released at the April conference in Maputo listed the countries most affected as Algeria, Angola, Burundi, Congo-Brazzaville, the Democratic Republic of Congo, Liberia, Rwanda, Sierra Leone, Sudan, and Uganda (Ali-Dinar). While some youth volunteer to join the armed forces, driven by economic need, personal choice or the search for adventure, many more are forced into service.

The most alarming escalation, however, involves even younger children, some as young as seven. The first documented systematic use of this tactic was by the South African-backed Mozambican National Resistance (Renamo) in the war in Mozambique in the 1980s. Particularly in southern Mozambique, where there were few adult men in the countryside to supply Renamo's forced recruitment at gunpoint, children came to make up a large proportion of the rebel force. Renamo commanders acknowledged that children were "easier to control" and less likely to succeed in deserting.

A 1991 study of displaced children in Mozambique found that 28 percent of children abducted by Renamo were trained for combat (Boothby). In the south, the average age of those trained was 11.5 years old. While children were often used for noncombat missions, they also took part in combat and in carrying out atrocities.

In more recent years, very young children have been used for combat and for atrocities against civilians by the Lord's Resistance Army rebels in Uganda and by rebels in Sierra Leone. The Liberian civil war featured extensive use of children by several of the contending forces. So does the current conflict in the Democratic Republic of the Congo.

Brutalization of child soldiers is sometimes an explicit part of their training. When a 12- or 13-year-old recruit has been forced to kill—sometimes even a family member or neighbor—the traumatic experience may serve as a kind of initiation. Believing they will be ostracized for their deed, children who have killed may be bound psychologically to the military group that has forcibly recruited them.

After a conflict has ended, reintegration of child soldiers adds to the already staggering costs of recovery. Those who have worked to rehabilitate child soldiers say they often exhibit profound psychological trauma and inability to adjust to normal life, at levels exceeding that of adult soldiers. Furthermore, children who have spent their key growing years in combat in the bush lack the skills they would normally have acquired in school or from older relatives. They most often face unemployment, with criminal activity among the few possibilities for survival as an adult.

Why Children Fight

Children are being denied their basic rights of simply being a carefree child and enjoying their childhood by attending school, playing with friends and developing in a secure environment. Unfortunately, many children, worldwide, are abducted from their homes and are forced to join military forcers, either it be government or rebel forces, at gunpoint. These children are traumatized, vulnerable and forced into committing horrific acts of violence, simply to ensure their own survival. Poverty, injustice, displacement, lack of access to education and the proliferation of small arms are just some of the factors

51

that contribute towards the recruitment of children as soldiers. In addition to, children not having outside responsibilities, which inhibit them from becoming child soldiers, unlike their adult counterparts (Maier).

Military commanders prefer children because of their emotional and physical immaturity, which enables them to be easily manipulated or 'brain washed' into the 'perfect soldier'. If they are not taught, young children are unable to correctly distinguish between right and wrong, in addition to this, children will carry out orders without questions because they are not aware of the consequences of their actions. The fact is that these children have no other choice when it comes to committing these acts of violence (Ibid). Under the influence of drugs, these children can be easily changed into heartless killers, with no notion of the acts that they commit when carrying out orders. During the majority of the time, especially before fighting, these children are under the influence of such drugs as; marijuana, amphetamines, crack cocaine or even a deadly 'home made' cocktail made from gunpowder and other local substances. These drugs make the children fearless for combat, even more so than adults, because these children are also trained to feel no emotions when it comes to murder, either it be the enemy or an innocent civilian. These children show no mercy (Sebelebele).

Children are the 'perfect soldier' for military commanders because of these following qualities; endurance, the ability to survive on both little food and water, they accept and carry out orders, generally without questions. Therefore, children were usually forced into such dangers as the frontlines of open conflict or either sent ahead of other troops to ensure that possible minefields were safe, while in rare cases children have also been used in suicide missions. In addition to this, the majority of child soldiers have transformed their situation in the war into a kind of game, because they are unable to fully comprehend or accept the real consequences that war can inflict. In a way, by making the war into a game it is a coping mechanism for these children (Maier). Orphans and refugee children are the must vulnerable for recruitment by military forces. This is because they are the most insecure due to them being poor and having no family support. Therefore, they are the least likely to escape from the military force. The military some times bribe Police officers to find and recruit children. These children are either taken off the streets or abducted from their homes, schools or communities, which sadly is very common throughout the continent. Military commanders, however, have also ensured that abducted children have no reason to escape by forcing them to commit violent atrocities against their own families and friends as well as their community. If children actually do try to escape from the military forces then they are hunted down and killed (Human Rights Watch).

Generally, children are seen as easily replaceable soldiers and of little worth by adult soldiers, this explains why so many children died needlessly. Military commanders kill children for the following reasons; if they refused to join the military force or carry out orders, if they became sick or can not keep up with their adult comrades and also for trying to escape. Some children, who ventured to do any of the previous, are considered very lucky if they are not killed, instead they are punished with terrible beatings or lashes form either their military commanders or even from their fellow comrades (Amnesty International).

> "Children all over the continent have willingly or unwillingly exchanged their school pens and pencils for rifles and hand grenades to become the ultimate representatives of a lost generation."—Karl Maier.

Children Committing Political Violence

Mohammed Kuteh, a former child soldier and elementary school boy from Sierra Leone writes about his experiences, "Most of these children are under the ages of 18 and are used as tools by the politicians and other elderly people in their society in order to fight for or against the government. Most of these children were separated from their parents. They have been trained in the bush and become very dangerous like wild animals"—they are violent!

"They use their weapons to launch a barrage of attacks on highways, towns and villages and seemingly every corner of their country. They also use weapons like machetes and knives that are used to amputate and inject the stomachs of pregnant women." He goes on to say, "They challenge themselves over the pregnant woman's stomach by saying that the unborn baby is a boy or girl so by this way they slit the stomach of the woman with crude knives and uproot the unborn baby." The irony of this story leaps out—children murdering unborn children, as if to subconsciously ensure that the baby will not have to endure this horror.

The story continues, "Some of these child soldiers also like burning houses, while dancing as the flames go up. They like killing innocent civilians while others like to rape pregnant women and highly educated women in the community. I am of course talking about (child soldiers who are boys}. Some child soldiers, particular the rebel child soldier, will ask their peers who they capture to kill their fathers or mothers. If anyone refuses to take their command, they will kill that person., but if the captive kills his mother, he or she is asked to drink the blood. To some bad extent, the body is prepared for them to eat as meat. They loot valuable properties that make them quarrel most times over the vulture practice. The quarrel leads them to shoot and kill each other and other innocent civilians around them."

"Finally, I think that the great violence and involvement of children in armed conflicts must be stopped immediately because if child soldiers are not stopped in such conflicts and war, there will be no peaceful atmosphere for the others growing up tomorrow. The only thing that the governments and other local and international non-governmental organizations should do is to create disarmament, demobilization and resettlement programs in order to integrate these children into society again."

West African Child Soldiers

The phenomenon of child soldiers in Côte d'Ivoire is clearly linked to non-resolved issues in Liberia. It is the result of previous failures to properly demobilize. In Liberia, only 4,300 child soldiers were demobilized (Amnesty International, 2005). With the end of the war in Liberia, former child soldiers often became street children that the civilian population would continue to fear. The temptation to go back to military life for them is strong. Many fighters from previous wars have "recycled" themselves to continue the cycle of war. Weak State authority and lack of law enforcement officers are also great incentive to cross porous borders into Côte d'Ivoire.

In Liberia children continue to be the main victims of conflicts. Their suffering takes many forms. Children are killed, made orphans, maimed, abducted, deprived of education and health care, and left with deep emotional scars and trauma. Forced to flee from their homes, refugees and internally displaced children are especially vulnerable to violence, recruitment, sexual exploitation, disease, malnutrition and death. Children are being recruited and used as child soldiers on a massive scale. Girls face additional risks, particularly sexual violence. These egregious violations of children's rights take place in a pervasive climate of impunity (UN Document, 2003).

The children of Liberia have suffered devastatingly the deprivations enumerated by the United Nations (UN) Secretary-General, Kofi Annan, in his most recent report to the UN Security Council on children and armed conflict. One of the most urgent challenges as Liberia emerges from protracted internal armed conflict is to respond adequately to the needs of the very large number of children under the age of eighteen years who have had their lives blighted by the violence and destruction that has racked Liberia almost continuously since late 1989. They have been denied their most fundamental rights, including their rights to family life, food, health and education.

CHAPTER 6

CONCLUSION

A. CURRENT US STRATEGY IN WEST AFRICA

Finally, and perhaps most challenging of all, there is the threats that arise from deepening economic and political crises in key African states. The brew of religious tension, economic deprivation, declining law and order and political instability could open this part of western Africa to some of the most serious forms of political violence and terrorist activity. The Council on Foreign Relations in 2005 said, "In fact in all parts of sub-Saharan Africa, our response to the political violence threat must be a broadly based one, bringing political, economic, and sensitive public diplomacy assets to bear. There was a telling moment in this regard during last year's crisis over Liberia. As rebel forces approached the capital, African and European nations alike urged the U.S. to provide troops on the ground to stabilize the situation. The UK had done so in neighboring Sierra Leone, France in Côte d'Ivoire."

"The President sent 3,000 Marines offshore of Liberia, but after a few days and after only a few troops had gone on shore for a short while, the troop ship sailed away. The President said that our primary interest had been that food and medicine could be provided, and once that was done our job was largely done. However one judges the desirability of providing American troops in that situation, the conclusion that our primary interest in a failing state, where once al Qaeda had reaped fortunes in diamond trading, was humanitarian was unfortunate. Our interest in Africa must be seen as strategic. Once that fundamental recognition takes place, the resources that will be needed can be judged accordingly. And only then will we meet the totality of the terrorist threat on the continent." If the United States does not view political violence in West Africa as a strategic problem, for the United States, then the probability that the United States will involve itself in this geographic region on any great scale is slight. What defines the United States' strategic outlook? The National Security Strategy characterizes those things that the United States holds important strategically and it will use its instruments of power to achieve. Diplomatic sway, information ability, military might and economic persuasion all are the instruments of power with which the United States uses to see its strategic goals achieved

National Security Strategy for Africa

The National Security Strategy (NSS) of September 2002 outlines what the strategic goals are for the United States. No document or policy can foresee every circumstance that the United States may be involved in; the Unites States does have finite political, economic, and military resources to meet its global priorities. The NSS outlines these two principles as a way to approach each case:

The United States should invest time and resources into building international relationships and institutions that can help manage local crises when they emerge.

The United States should be realistic about its ability to help those who are unwilling or unready to help themselves. Where and when people are ready to do their part, we will be willing to move decisively.

President George Bush describes Africa as, "Promise and opportunity sit side by side with disease, war, and desperate poverty. This threatens both a core value of the United States— preserving human dignity—and our strategic priority—combating global terror." In this thesis I have shown that there are indeed very close parallels between

58

terrorism and political violence, particularly how both of these perpetuations of violence often affect noncombatants. It would then seem that what is known of political violence and, according to George Bush, what the core values of the Unites States are, that there are indeed linkages and justifications that the Unites States must be strategically involved in Africa. He goes on to say in the NSS, "American interests and American principles, therefore, lead in the same direction: we will work with others for an African continent that lives in liberty, peace, and growing prosperity. Together with our European allies, we must help strengthen Africa's fragile states, help build indigenous capability to secure porous borders, and help build up the law enforcement and intelligence infrastructure to deny havens for terrorists."

World leaders and European colonialists drew present-day African country borders over a century ago. They gave no mind to tribal boundaries, ethnic kingdoms and realms. It is no wonder that today many regional African conflicts rarely know any bonds to its capacity. As the CH model predicted in the case studies and as the NSS states, "lethal environments exist in Africa as local civil wars spread beyond borders to create regional war zones. Forming coalitions of the willing and cooperative security arrangements are key to confronting these emerging transnational threats."

Achieving bilateral engagement and building coalitions of the willing will focus the NSS goals for Africa. Along with the principles mentioned above the three interlocking strategies that must be applied to Africa according to the NSS are as follows:

- Countries with major impact on their neighborhood such as South Africa, Nigeria, Kenya, and Ethiopia are anchors for regional engagement and require focused attention;

- Coordination with European allies and international institutions is essential for constructive conflict mediation and successful peace operations; and

- Africa's capable reforming states and sub-regional organizations must be strengthened as the primary means to address transnational threats on a sustained basis.

Because of the focus for this thesis, the regional player in West Africa is Nigeria. The NSS lauds Nigeria as an "anchor" for the region; to me this may be an overstatement. I agree that focused attention is needed for Nigeria. I believe, however, that the attention must be given only to prevent Africa's most populous country from falling into economic and ethnic chaos that, if ignored by the AU and developed countries would absolutely plummet the LCS countries into economic turmoil, and therefore civil turmoil, the likes Africa has never before experienced. The NSS states, "Ultimately the path of political and economic freedom presents the surest route to progress in sub-Saharan Africa, where most wars are conflicts over material resources and political access often tragically waged on the basis of ethnic and religious difference." This statement is very telling and accurate and may be the one statement in the entire NSS that boils the strife in Africa down to a single explanatory concept. Political violence is perpetrated because of material gain and, by definition, for political access. It is those that are caught in the foray of the pursuit of economic and political freedom that are the noncombatants about which I speak in this thesis.

B. THE UNITED STATES' COMMITMENT TO CURB POLITICAL VIOLENCE IN WEST AFRICA

In virtually every conflict situation in Africa today, the credibility of the US government's words and deeds is questioned. American diplomats are hamstrung by the US domestic climate of disengagement, which has produced a decline in the attention given to these conflicts by senior officials and in the institutional and resource capabilities that would facilitate US engagement. Overcoming declining US credibility, analysts suggest, is not just a matter of reversing the disengagement trend, but is also a matter of devising innovative ways to deal with new types of problems that armed conflicts, that perpetuate political violence, in Africa pose. Disengagement from Africa affects US interests in a number of tangible ways. It undermines US claims to global leadership, results in lost opportunities for trade and investment ties, may jeopardize access to critical strategic minerals, and inhibits the ability to stave off environmental disasters that can have global consequences. Moreover, the United States has a humanitarian interest in saving lives and preventing, or refusing to tolerate, genocide.

The principal challenge for US policy in "failed" or failing states such as Liberia and Côte d'Ivoire is how to provide an appropriate blend of incentives toward more peaceful interaction and disincentives toward violence; most importantly violence in the name of political ends that encapsulates noncombatants. The challenge in Liberia is no longer one of early warning and preventive action—but one of containing violence and preventing escalation to the point of spillover into neighboring fragile states such as Guinea and Sierra Leone. In the absence of extensive official US engagement and easily identifiable traditional levers of influence, the UN, NGOs and private diplomacy have helped fill the vacuum. In situations such as those in Liberia and Sierra Leone, dealing effectively with the injustices of the past is critical to breaking the culture of impunity that provides incentives for violence. Truth commissions, such as South Africa has been successful in establishing, and other transitional justice mechanisms such as international criminal tribunals can often have "demonstration" effects in neighboring states—i.e., they

61

show that severe human rights abuses may eventually lead to punishment. Charles Taylor, upon hearing that he had been indicted on war crimes charges by the International Court (held in Sierra Leone) fled the country and took up exile in Nigeria. This message had great impact upon neighboring states that, in fact, international law does mean something.

Even when peace agreements are reached, their implementation is by no means ensured. Liberia's most recent strife is a case of the implementation of a peace agreement gone awry. There is an urgent need to renegotiate the Abuja agreement, Liberia's most recent peace accord, and to solve the critical problem of warlordism. If one were to introspectively look at each of Liberia's previous presidents one would find that they were all former warlords—all of which systematically engaged in political violence targeting noncombatants on their quest for political power. A critical current concern among policymakers is how to reconfigure the West African peacekeeping force ECOMOG in such a way that it can contribute to stabilizing the situation in Liberia.

C. CONCLUSION

There are ways for the United States to continue promoting the cessation of political violence in an environment of economic strife, civil war and the threat of terrorism: create trade and investment incentives for peace, back NGO and private peacemaking efforts, enhance cooperation with US allies, and further strengthen African and regional conflict management capabilities.

United States' policymakers should take a closer look at the actual and potential role of foreign (particularly U.S.) investors in promoting peace (or contributing to conflict) in Africa, and, relatedly, the role of international financial institutions in supporting conflict management as an element of structural adjustment and development programs. It can certainly be argued that where economic prosperity and democracy are found, so too can be found state political systems that work for the people and do not violently engage against it. The CH model details many variables like social, ethnic and religious fractionalization that cause a state to inwardly implode through the vehicle of civil war. With strong US engagement in West Africa these factors become less important because the average family then begins to realize that the pursuit of life, liberty and happiness can be universal and it not reserved only for those that wield guns or vie for political power.

The future of US engagement in Africa in promoting conflict management will increasingly depend on the ability of proponents of such engagement to clearly articulate not only US interests in the continent, but also how various policies and tools aimed at conflict management can have a demonstrable impact on furthering those interests. Political violence against noncombatants occurs because of the recipe that the countries of LCS have cooked up. Child soldiers, economic deprivation and civil war all contribute to this end. The US, as the champion of those that are oppressed, must understand what causes noncombatants to get caught in the middle of this kind of violence. Through engagement and assistance to this region of Africa will political violence be routed and hopefully dismissed to allow its citizens those freedoms and life privileges that we so enjoy.

GLOSSARY

Al-Qaeda. Global terrorist network led by Usama bin Laden

Blood Diamonds. Those diamonds that are misappropriated and the proceeds from their sale is used to finance corruption, political violence and terrorism.

Charles Taylor. Dictator of Liberia from July of 1997 to June 4, 2003.

Diaspora. The dispersion of an ethnic people away from its original homeland.

Hypothesis. A tentative explanation for observed events.

Ingratiated. Gain favor, "suck up" to

Koran. The book of Islam, holy teachings of the Prophet Muhammad

Shari'a. Arabic for 'Islamic law.'

State terrorism. State terrorism is defined by some as violence upon a population committed by national governments or their proxies when not in a state of armed conflict with that population.

West. Represents the developed, non-Muslim countries of Europe and North America

REFERENCE LIST

Ali-Dinar, Ali B. *Maputo Conference to Seek End to the Use of Children as Soldiers in Africa.* Accessed 30 March 2005 at http://www.africa.upenn.edu/Hornet/irin_4799a.html.

Amnesty International. *Childhood denied: child soldiers in Africa.* Accessed on 4 April 2005 at http://web.amnesty.org/web/web.nsf/print/childsoldiers-africanchild-eng

Ashby, Phil. 2003. *Escape from Sierra Leone.* St. Martin's Paperbacks.

Booth, Wayne C., Gregory G. Colomb and Joseph M. Williams. 1995. *The Craft of Research.* The University of Chicago Press.

Boothby, Neil. *Children of Mozambique.* Save the Children Federation. 1988.

Bush, George W. 2001. The Global War on Terrorism: The First 100 Days. *The White House.* The Coalition Information Centers October, 3-8.

Bush, George W. 2002. *National Security Strategy of the United States of America.* Washington, DC: The White House.

Bush, George W. 2003. *National Strategy for Combating Terrorism.* Washington, DC: The White House.

Bush, George W. 2005. *National Military Strategy of the United States of America.* Washington, DC: The White House.

Campbell, Kurt M., Michele A. Flournoy. 2001. *To Prevail: An American Strategy for the Campaign Against Terrorism.* Washington DC: The CSIS Press

Child-soldiers.org accessed on 20 March 2005 at www.child-soldiers.org.

Collier, Paul and Anke Hoeffler. 2000. *On the Incidence of Civil War in Africa.* World Bank Policy Research Working Paper, Washington D.C.

Collier, Paul and Anke Hoeffler. 2000. *Greed and Grievance in Civil War*, presented at conference on the economics of political violence, Princeton University, 18-19 March 2000.

Collier, Paul. 2000. *Doing Well Out of War: An Economic Perspective*, in Mats Berdal and David M. Malone (eds.), pp. 91-112

Council on Foreign Relations. Princeton N. Lyman. *Fighting Terrorism in Africa.* Testimony before the House Committee on International Relations

Subcommittee on Africa, April 1, 2004 accessed 23 April 2005 at
http://www.cfr.org.

Dukule, Abdoulaye W. *The Last Friend on the Block....* The Perspective accessed at
http://www.theperspective.org/ouagadougou.html on 5 May 2005.

Gunaratna, Rohan. 2002. *Inside Al-Qaeda: Global Network of Terror.* New York:
Columbia University Press, March

Hübschle, Annette. 2004. *Unholy Alliance.* Accessed 11 February 2005 at
http://www.iss.org.za/pubs/papers/93/93.pdf.

Huhtala, Ambassador Marie T. 2003. Remarks to the Rotary International Dinner Forum.
Kuala Lumpur, Malaysia.

Human Rights Watch. *Facts about Child Soldiers.* 2004. Accessed 15 March 2005 at
http://www.humanrightswatch.org/campaigns/crp/facts.htm

ILO.org. Accessed on 19 March 2005 at www.ilo.org.

Kaplan, Robert D. 2000. *The Coming Anarchy.* Random House, New York.

Keen, David. Transcript of speech accessed at
http://www.crisisstates.com/News/terrorism(keen).htm on 12 December 2004.

Lake, Anthony. 2000. *6 Nightmares: Real Threats in a Dangerous World and How
America Can Meet Them.* New York, Brown and Company

Maier, Karl. *Into the House of the Ancestors.* John Wiley & Sons. New York, 1998. pp
132.

Manwaring, Max G. 2002. The Inescapable Global Security Arena, Strategic Studies
Institute, PA: US Army War College, April

Mazrui, Ali A. 1999. *Comparative Acts of War: A Personal View* accessed at
http://www.swahilionline.com/features/articles/mazrui/prof%20mazrui.htm on 27
November 2004.

McCullough, Colin; Huang, Reyko. 2002. "In the Spotlight: JI" Center for Defense
Information, October 18, available at www.cdi.org/terrorism/ji-pr.cfm

Merriam-Webster Online Dictionary at http://www.merriam-webster.com/ accessed on 7
January 2005.

Nagbe, Blatu. 2001. *Are We Really Waging a War Against Terrorism?* Accessed 12
December 2004 at
http://www.awitness.org/news/november_2001/african_terror_ignored.html

Nathan, Laurie. 2000. *The Four Horsemen of the Apocalypse: The Structural Causes of Crisis and Violence in Africa*, Peace and Change, Vol. 25, No. 2, pp. 190-19.

Office of the Coordinator for Counter-Terrorism. 2004. Patterns of Global Terrorism 2003: East Asia. Department of State, April 29.

Osei, Albert Wireko. *Protectionism: Africa's Perennial Headache.* Accra Mail, 9 July 2002. Accessed at http://www.globalpolicy.org/socecon/ffd/2002/0709protectionism.htm on 7 April 2005.

Perl, Raphael F. 2001. *Terrorism, the Future, and U.S. Foreign Policy.* Congressional Research Service . The Library of Congress.

Sambanis, Nicholas. 2003. *Using Case Studies to Expand the Theory of Civil War.* CPR Working Papers, Paper No. 5.

Scobell, Andrew. 2002. "Defeating Terrorism: Strategic Issue Analyses" Strategic Studies Institute, PA: US Army War College

Sebelebele, Matome. *Child Soldiers Remain a Challenge for African Union.* African News Service. July 2002, pp 1-2.

United Nations Document. *Children and Armed Conflict.* Report of the Secretary-Genera, A/58/546-S/2003/1053, 10 November 2003, para.24.

World Bank Group. The Economics of Civil Wars, Crime and Violence. Accessed at http://www.worldbank.org/research/conflict/ on 3 January 2005.

www.ingramcontent.com/pod-product-compliance
Lightning Source LLC
Chambersburg PA
CBHW080524290526
45790CB00006B/2302